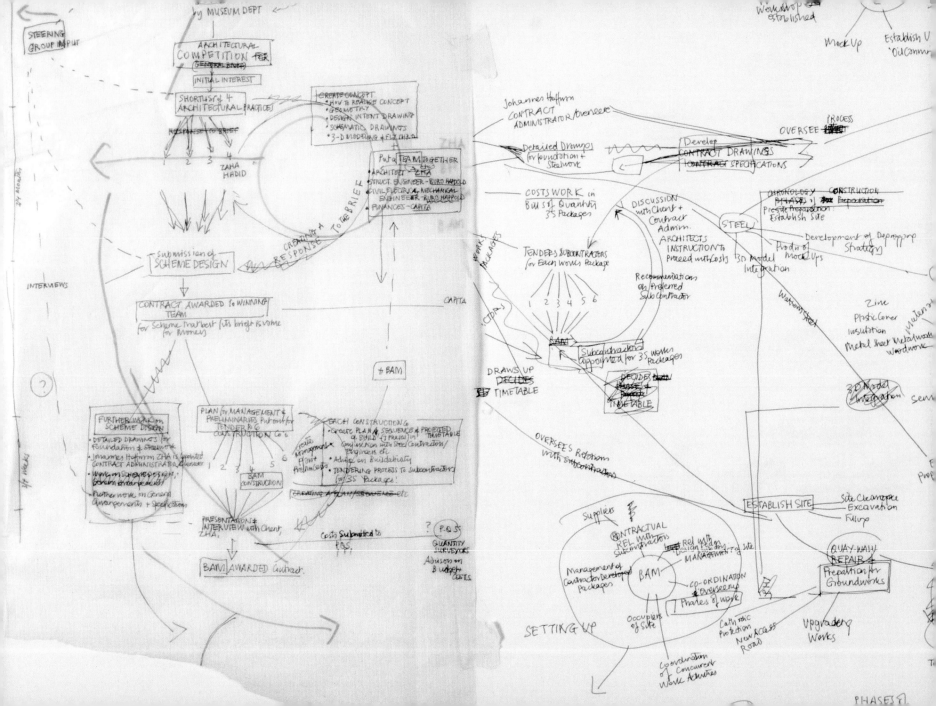

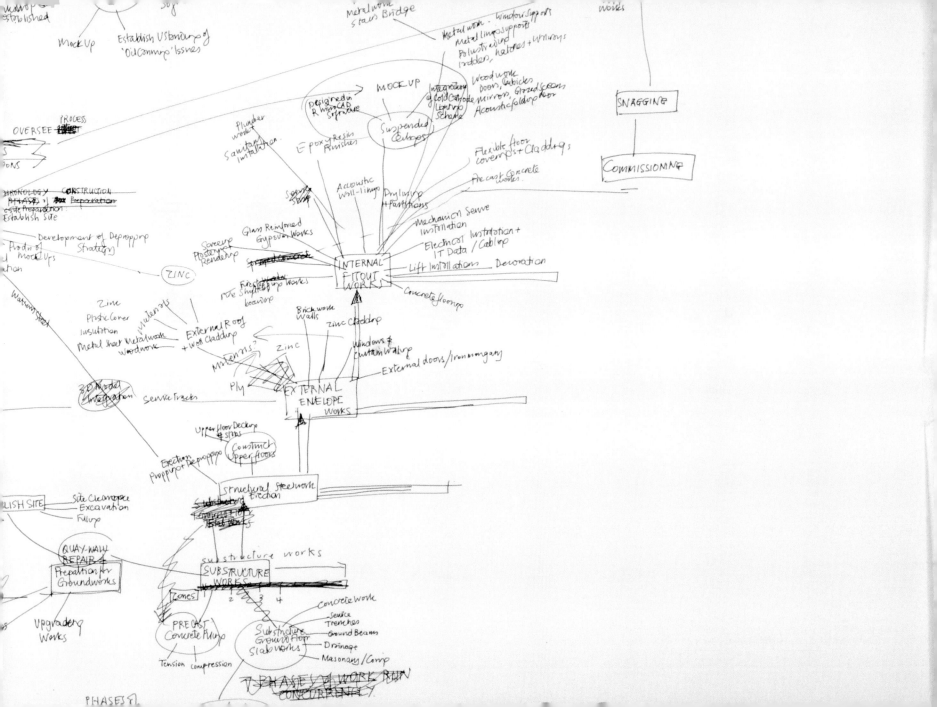

MockUp established

MockUp

Establish USbnding of 'OilConmp' Issues

Metalwork Stairs Bridge

Metal work - Window Supports Metal linings supports Balustrading Ironmongery Ladders, hatches + walkways

MOCK UP

Woodwork doors, Cubicles mirrors, Glazed Screens Acoustic folding door

SNAGGING

Designed in R himCAD software

Integrated array of Cold Cathode Lighting Scheme

Suspended Ceilings

OVERSEE PROCESS

Plumber works Sanitation installation

Epoxy Resin Finishes

Flexible floor coverings + Claddings

COMMISSIONING

Precast Concrete works.

DRONOLOGY CONSTRUCTION PHASES) Preparation Site preparation Establish Site

Acoustic Wall-linings

Drylining +Partitions

Mechanical Serve Installation

Development of Depropping Strategy

Production of Mock Ups

ZINC

Service Screed

Glass Reinforced Gypsum Works

Severe Plastering Rendering

INTERNAL FITOUT WORKS

Electrical Installation + IT Data / Cabling

Lift Installations   Decoration

Fire Shuttering Works boarding

Concrete floorings

Waterproofing

Zinc Plastic Coner Insulation Metal Sheet Metalwork Woodwork

Materials

Brickwork Walls

Zinc Cladding

External Roof + Wall Cladding

Windows & Curtain Walling

3D Model Integration

Materials?

Zinc

Ply

EXTERNAL ENVELOPE Works

External doors/Ironmongery

Service Tracks

Upper Floor Decking & slabs

Construct Upper floors

Erection Propping & Depropping?

Structural Steelwork Erection

LISH SITE

Site Clearance Excavation Fill up

Substructure Ground Floor Slab Works

QUAY-WALL REPAIR Preparation for Groundworks

substructure works

SUBSTRUCTURE WORKS

Zones   2 3 4

Concrete Work

Upgrading Works

PRECAST Concrete Piling

Substructure Ground Floor Slab Works

Service Trenches Ground Beams Drainage Masonary/Comp

Tension compression

PHASES OF WORK RUN CONCURRENTLY

PHASES

Kelvingrove Art Gallery & Museum
15TH April – 14TH August 2011

Patricia Cain:
Drawing (on) Riverside

Edited by Rowena Murray

Contributors
Neil Baxter
Patricia Cain
James Cosgrove
Alan Dunlop
Alec Galloway
Zaha Hadid
Lorens Holm
Ian Johnston
Rosalind Lawless
Phil Lavery
Rowena Murray
Ann Nisbet
Anne Perry
Steve Rigley
Hugh Stevenson

(previous page) A working schematic
drawing showing the process of
construction of the Riverside Museum.

Patricia Cain:

Drawing (on) Riverside

Construction sites / Constructing sites
Patricia Cain

By observing a building as it is being built in drawings and paintings, you're capturing a moment in time, but as part of that, you can't help but learn about the processes you're recording. Pretty soon I realised through this observationally-based work that I was interrogating the interactions of the processes used on-site and the relationships between the contractors involved. Because of this, I wanted to make these creative and collaborative processes of making the focus for the exhibition: I wanted to explore process through process rather than look at the building as an artefact through a series of highly finished objects.

My on-site observations highlighted the 'give and take' nature of the collaborative process of construction, and early on I decided I wanted to push this through a small range of architectural and model-making collaborations with other practitioners and get others to respond to the building through the work I have done in the past few years.

The idea quickly became to expose the creative processes between us all and record how the progression of our discoveries was worked through. By doing this, I began to make connections between the activities used to create this building and those previously used on this particular site, which was formerly a shipyard.

Each collaboration has been a different experience, influenced by the relationships between our different disciplines, working methods and personalities. I set out to work with people I knew and felt I could trust, and although each collaboration had to navigate difficult issues of funding, methods of working, each other's timetables, and matters of authorship and territory of expertise, we managed to productively and positively see things through. The fact that I've had to trespass on other people's practices as part of this process has given us all an insight into our own styles and methods by comparison to those of others.

For the staff at Kelvingrove, who are more accustomed to planning objects and interpretations well in advance of exhibitions, our collaboration on a project where the final form and content for exhibition evolved only as our making processes evolved, must have sometimes seemed a rather hazardous experience. Our collaboration has in effect been the process of constructing the exhibition, in which the artist has been allowed to be the architect or 'project manager'.

This has required a great deal of faith, not least because those in other disciplines (including those involved in the written and designed aspects of this publication), experienced a plight familiar to the artist – that of not being able to say what you're doing until you've done it.

Activities like this which are skill-led rather than concept-led, where one is working blind to a certain extent and where intuition is a major mode of development, often create this curious relationship between theorising and making, which as Dunlop says, is why drawing and making are so important.

I strongly suspect this process of finding through making has been familiar in the collaboration between Zaha Hadid Architects, Bruro Happold, and Bam Construction (amongst others) during the Museum's construction. I know, for instance, that making physical models became a significant part of the construction process when the non-parallel lines of the geometry of the building could not be read in sections of the drawn plans.

In retrospect, I could perhaps now say that the exhibition has two formative bases: one that is practical – the interrogation of things by making – and one that is conceptual – the building site as a place of questioning, progress and exchange[1]. In effect, I've been pushing this exploratory work through the exhibition and making visible the construction of the idea through the emerging artefact.

1. I acknowledge these ideas have also been addressed by a recent project at the Architectural Association.

(above and right) Construction of
the Architectural Installation.
Kelvingrove (March 2011)

The Exhibition – A Work in Progress
Anne Perry

This is the first exhibition of its type to be exhibited in any of our venues. What sets it apart is that it is a work in progress, and its main theme is the recording of a work in progress: the construction of the Riverside Museum on the River Clyde. We usually mount exhibitions of completed works, but in this case, we are working alongside the artist and developing the exhibition with her. We usually know which objects we are going to display, but in this exhibition we do not know exactly what we are going to get. Some pieces will be constructed during the installation period, just weeks before the opening date.

What makes this exhibition even more interesting – and risky – is that while Cain is primarily a painter, in this project she is working with other artists and specialists to produce a huge variety of work in different media, which means that some of it is new to her. This was risky for both her and us, but we have built up a relationship of trust throughout the project and have been communicating on an almost daily basis.

As a result of Cain's approach, this exhibition shows the dynamic relationships between art, architecture and industry and examines the processes of each. Cain's work encapsulates the process of regeneration through construction and the links between the river and the urban environment. Her work responds to the process of the regeneration in Glasgow and Clydeside, through art, by recording the construction of a building that is sure to become a Glasgow icon. Cain's art builds on the past but looks to the future.

Forensic Examination:
Studies of Evolving Form

James Cosgrove

The process of investigation

This body of work is a sustained, almost 'forensic', examination of the development of a fine example of modern architectural design and construction methods, where the focus of the artist is on the seemingly organic processes employed by the builders, as much as the growing and resultant structure – both in a visual sense and as an analysis of that fleeting symbiotic relationship.

Resisting quick or easy results, Cain wrestles with ideas about drawing which are rooted in acute observation and investigation, driven by the urge to understand complex physical and inter-relational circumstances.

Seldom purely pictorially driven, the drawings explore the interaction between the complex and temporary (at times apparently, reactive or 'ad hoc') form of amalgamated scaffolding and roof support structures against the evolving permanent form with its skeletal framework and layers of skins.

The result of this painstaking process is, for the artist, an enhanced understanding of three-dimensional phenomena and its annotation or depiction onto an unyielding flat surface. But the creative process is never quite as simple or linear as this suggests, given, in this case, the transient nature of the supporting structures for construction and monitoring purposes – and evidence of human engagement – and the emergent, permanent form that evolves from layers of materials, processes and meaning.

Each of Cain's finished drawings and paintings is the culmination of gathering together many hundreds of on-site sketches and visual references, notes and conversations, all underpinned by extensive research into technical factors, historical context and precedents – a live and opportunistic exploration of architectural metamorphosis.

The legacy for the viewer is to discover (or have uncovered by the artist) exciting dynamic relationships in graphic form and colour; order where there might initially appear randomness (or carefully orchestrated chaos); insight into the selective and editorial process for abstracted pictorial purposes – rich aesthetic pickings – even from the most unlikely of starting points.

The triptych

Cain's use of the triptych seems an appropriate method of subdividing an expansive architectural space (the conjoined picture plane), with its myriad activities and forms, into distinct but related frames. Similar, in a way, to a panning shot in a film, it suggests an animated drama in both set (temporary structures) and theatre (the building).

Other works and an evolving practice

Many smaller pieces in the exhibition indicate possible points of departure for the artist, and the direction this may take could be rooted in these more minimalist works.

Where much of Cain's practice is concerned with depicting systems of construction and detailed built structures, works such as *Riverside Museum Interior No.1* and *Riverside Interior V* owe their integrity to a process of deconstruction. Collaged or painted shapes in seemingly arbitrary colour appear to simplify or deny form and perspective, and the reductive nature of the 'drawn' elements suggests structure or massing of forms without attempting to describe it as such.

Often drawings that explore objects within a perspectival space hint at breaking from restrictions of their own self-imposed two-dimensional artifice. Making three-dimensional presences would seem a natural step for an artist whose reflective practice is rooted in creatively edited representations of the constructed world and knows no bounds.

1.
Riverside Interior V (2010)
170 x 105cm pastel and acrylic
2.
Riverside Interior I (2009)
122 x 91.5cm pastel

2.

1.

Patricia Cain's place in Topographical Art in Glasgow
Hugh Stevenson

1.

2.

The Glasgow Museums topographical collection reflects the interest that artists have shown in the built environment of the city. Patricia Cain's work is a significant contribution to this continuing history.

The earliest representations were made principally as historical records of the growing and changing city. Captain John Slezer's engravings made at the end of the 17th century are a unique record of the areas around the Cathedral, the Old College and the River Clyde, although the aesthetic response of the artist is limited. In the mid-18th century artists of the short-lived Foulis Academy recorded the principal streets of the city and the Green, but their work smacks more of experimentation with the technique of etching than great art. In the mid-to-late 19th century a significant group of three artist/topographers actively set out to record for posterity the ancient and picturesque sights of the city before they fell prey to industrialisation. William Simpson is the outstanding artist of this period, with his meticulous attention to detail. He generally sought perfection in pinpoint accurate historical records, but occasionally showed demolition – as of the old medieval bridge – or reconstruction – such as the monumental river widening. Also a historian, he wrote the carefully researched commentaries that accompanied the collectors' edition book in which these drawings were reproduced. Thomas Fairbairn's drawings were reproduced as colour lithographs.

David Small recorded every last carved architectural or sculptural detail that he could find of old Glasgow.

At the start of the 20th century Muirhead Bone brought his revolutionary aesthetic response to the built environment of Glasgow, and is surely the greatest artist in this short study. Gone was the thirst for every last picturesque detail or historical remnant. Instead, Bone sought to interpret the raw power of structures in the process of creation or destruction as well as in their prime. The prison wall, the station gantry, wooden scaffolding or a demolition site could inspire in equal measure. Shipyards were heaven sent for Bone's pencil, etching needle or lithographic chalk.

In the first few decades of the 20th century artists catering to the 'black and white' obsession generally confined themselves to the sort of subject matter chosen by Simpson, Fairbairn and Small, rather than following Bone's lead. Occasionally, a shipyard or foundry would commission a portfolio such as Frank Mason's drypoints of Beardmore's works, with interesting results, but more often than not the safe option was chosen.

In the post-war period modernism and abstraction beckoned, and the theme was picturesque decay of canals, docks and tenements and the run-down areas favoured by Joan Eardley. School of Art students were particularly drawn to this sort of subject, which gave opportunities for self-expression

and experimentation in colour, shape and form.
The printmaking revival, led by the Glasgow Print
Studio, provided new opportunities for work of this
nature.

Patricia Cain represents a new direction in depicting the city – she draws and paints the renewal,
rather than the old, the picturesque or the desolate.
A worthy successor to Bone, she communicates
her personal reaction to the power of the new, the
monumental and the excitement of construction.

1.
Cornerstone (2011)
40 x 30cm etching
Patricia Cain

2.
Taking down the 'Auld Brig
William Simpson (1850) *pencil and watercolour*
Bought by Glasgow Museums, (1898)
Reproduced courtesy of the Artist's Estate

3.
Fairfield's Shipyard
Muirhead Bone. *From a portfolio of five lithographs*
Given to Glasgow Museums by Mr Mitchell, (1963)
Reproduced courtesy of the Artist's Estate

3.

1.
Riverside Scaffolding IV (2011)
140 x 122cm pastel
2.
Inscape II (2008)
105 x 170cm pastel
3.
Inscape III (2008)
105 x 170cm pastel

1.

2.

3.

1.

2.

1.
Laying Out (2011)
59 x 84cm pastel (detail)

2.
Zinc Fold (2011)
84 x 59 cm pastel

3.
Riverside Scaffolding V (2011)
140 x 122cm pastel

3.

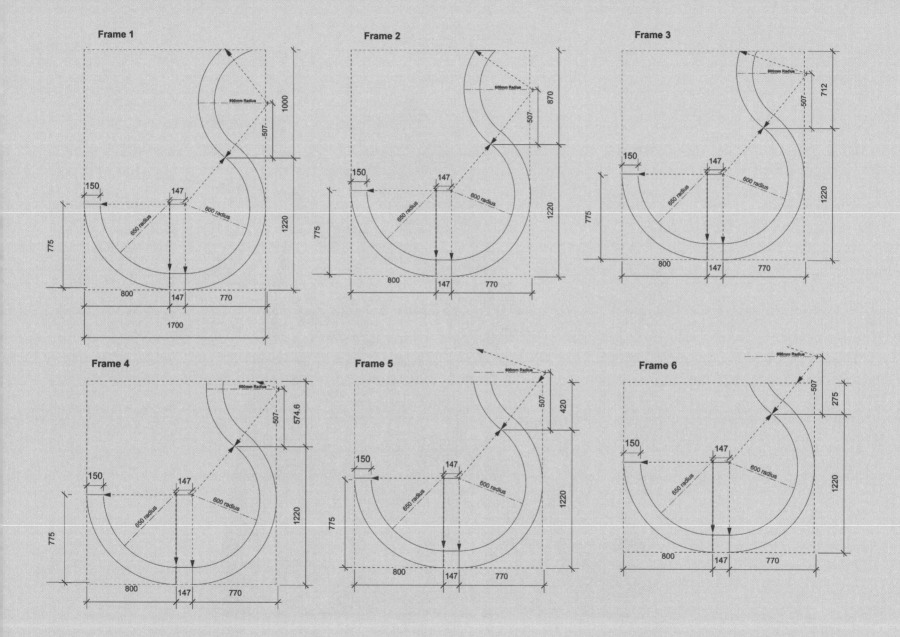

Collaboration Through Research

Ann Nisbet

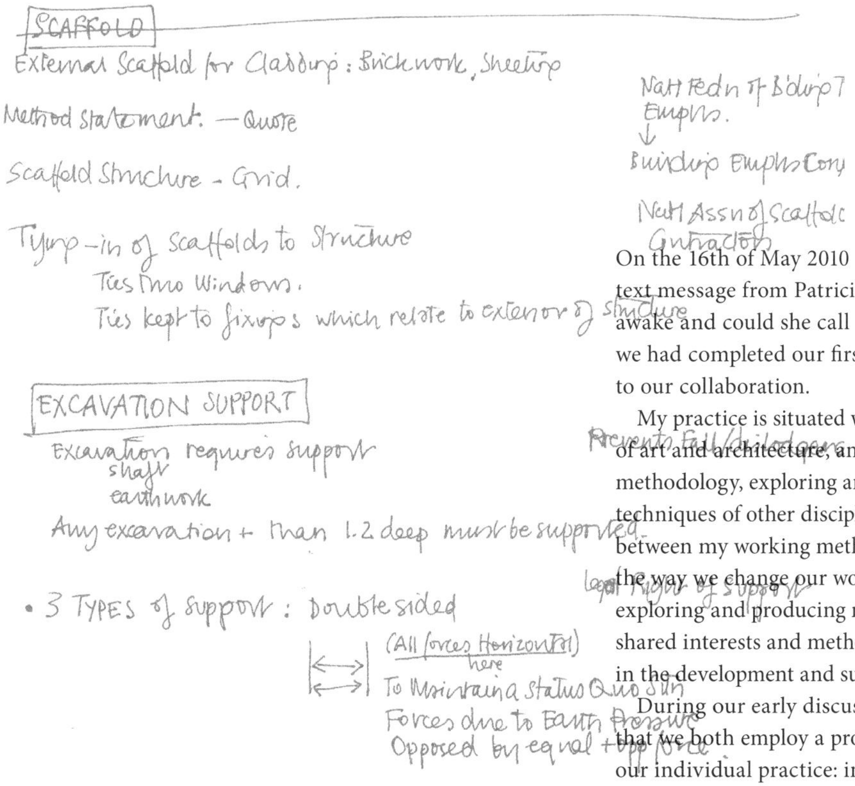

Handwritten notes (left column):

SCAFFOLD

External Scaffold for Cladding: Brickwork, Sheeting

Method statement. — Quote

Scaffold Structure - Grid.

Tying-in of scaffolds to Structure

Ties thro Windows.

Ties kept to fixings which relate to exterior of structure

EXCAVATION SUPPORT

Excavation requires support
    shaft
    earthwork

Any excavation + than 1.2 deep must be supported.

• 3 TYPES of support : Double sided

(All forces Horizontal)
    here
To Maintain a status Quo sun
Forces due to Earth Pressure
Opposed by equal + opp force

Natt Fed'n of B'ldng7
Emplrs.
↓
Building Emplrs Conf

Natt Assn of Scaffold
Contractors

Prevents Soil/building

legal right of support

On the 16th of May 2010 at 7.10am I received a text message from Patricia Cain asking if I was awake and could she call me. Thirty minutes later we had completed our first conversation relating to our collaboration.

My practice is situated within the boundaries of art and architecture, and employs a process-led methodology, exploring architecture through the techniques of other disciplines. There is a similarity between my working methods and Cain's and in the way we change our working process as a way of exploring and producing new work and ideas. These shared interests and methodologies were significant in the development and success of our collaboration.

During our early discussions it became apparent that we both employ a process of research within our individual practice: investigating through research, rather than reacting to an abstract concept. Documentation of early research took the form of a visual network, film, photographs, notes and the development of a method of rigorously interrogating the Riverside Museum's concept, site history and construction techniques.

We were in agreement that our installation would examine and respond to the processes used in the construction of the Riverside Museum, acknowledging that a research methodology would inform and dictate the direction of the work.

Drawing on our individual interests in documenting, specifically temporal processes, we began to investigate and research the temporary works within the construction of the museum, such as formwork, scaffolding and propping. The narrative and history of the site, which was once a shipyard, led us to draw comparisons and make connections between these methods and the traditional blocks, propping, and shoring associated with shipbuilding.

Our installation makes connections with temporal construction techniques employed on the Clyde, both past and present. The work responds to the contemporary steel propping and de-propping processes employed in the construction of the Museum and draws connections through the shared characteristics with shipbuilding.

The installation exposes the narrative, by making visible the ephemeral processes involved in both the Riverside Museum and shipbuilding, making the temporal permanent and the permanent temporal. It is not representational of either, but is a piece of work derived from the key elements of both.

The installation was not developed from an automatic response but from a deeper understanding of the subject. In a collaboration using a research methodology, several strands come together to create the work. There is the individual, there is the collaborator, and informing and linking the two is the research. The boundaries in ownership between collaborators become blurred, and the research deepens, reinforces, weaves and develops new ideas.

(opposite) detail drawings of frames for architectural installation. *Ann Nisbet*

Chronology of ideas arising during
the collaboration between Patricia Cain
and Ann Nisbet

29.07.10 *Thinking about how a concept is realised*

– Idea of coming to interrogate things just by starting
to make
– The building as work in progress – we like it when
the process is revealed, where both the construction
process and design ideas are revealed
– Construction = the realisation of the concept and
coming together of members of the collaboration,
the point where ideas are realised
– How? – we could start by producing a series of
small pieces of work, recording the making and
decisions as we make – photographs, writing, the
pieces themselves. The materials themselves could
be a constraint.

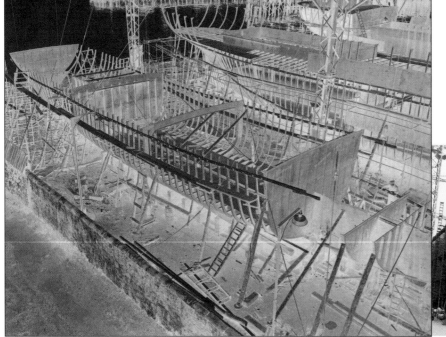

27.08.10 – *Possible options*

– Map the changing shape of the Clyde, particularly in relation to the shipyards
– Map the changes in the depth of the river and changes in ebb and flow as a consequence – how do you record something that's in motion all the time?
– Interrogate the idea that the concept for the Riverside works because it is site specific – links between the reflective properties of the river and the movement and flow of the building. The concept is found in different scales of the building.
– Interrogate through model-making the idea of nature of temporary structures and the nature of unfinishedness. Temporary elements are visible only through the process – it is a point when the process is exposed. (Connections between the temporary propping of the building, being 'on the stocks' during shipbuilding, and the propping of the quay walls as the Clyde was altered.)
– Unfinished things are more interesting – they expose the process
– Drawing on the research – the idea that research precedes everything: it brings depth to what we know and our ideas

23.09.10 *Taking from the construction of ships*

– Ships are made of standard components/geometry.
– We're interested in taking the forms of ships but applying them to different shapes – tailoring the usually standard components of ships and trying to apply them to a fluid geometry: standard widths that twist and turn.

1.
Riverside Wash (2011)
59 x 84cm ink
2.
Riverside Study III (2011)
74 x 61cm mixed media
3.
Building the Riverside Museum1
(2009) *140.5 x 105.5cm*
pastel & acrylic

1.

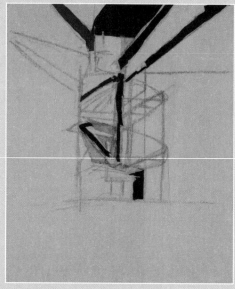

2.

3.

The Art of Process
Rowena Murray

Propping

Think of a process – drawing, building, writing – and you uncover things you don't usually think about consciously. Look at the steps in the process and you see things you don't normally see. They tell us more about the process and make us see it differently. This exhibition explains how a building was put together and why it looks and feels the way it does. It reveals the propping – the solid frames and underlying ideas – used in making it, helping us to see the lines, forms, trades, texts, moments and people that make the work what it is.

Making

Getting under the surface of a building – particularly a public building – is about sifting through a collection of ideas. We can no longer see the props and scaffolding that held it up and kept its shape, but this exhibition is scaffolding for the ideas that went into its making. Drawing, talking and writing about the building will continue, as we use it, as we get to know it and as we walk around this exhibition. The process of making the building will be the subject of conversations, arguments, reflections and interactions among visitors, critics and Glasgwegians for years to come.

Connecting

Trying to represent all the processes involved is not easy. Some parts of the process will be obscured; it's not possible to explain everything. The process of making – a ship or a building or a piece of writing – depends on collaborations between people and real connections between the processes they use. Trying to track all the connections between all the steps in the process and all the people who work on it is a complex task. Trying to capture everyone's perspective, at every stage in the process, is not easy, but the process of making something new involves understanding different versions of the process, while also trying to see it differently. This exhibition uses notebooks, discussions, transcripts and sketches to give us glimpses of what's going on in the process of making, but they don't tell the full story. They are merely props for our understanding of what's going on here. Looking for connections – are the steps in the process all in series, are the processes all connected? – is interesting too. Making connections – as we link steps in the process, connecting different processes – is an ongoing dialogue.

The art of process – process as art

Thinking about process can itself produce something new: a new perspective, a new step in the process, a better understanding of how we prop up the process of making. But the finished work – the ship, the building, the essay or the book – is not simply the output of a mechanical process; nor is the output always more important than the process. Clearly, the two are linked. This exhibition props up our viewing of the building. It shows that process both grows from and feeds outcome. It shows us that the process is as important as the finished work.

(above) **Riverside Framework** (2009)
122 x 91.5cm pastel and acrylic

(opposite)
Riverside Triptych II (2011)
170 x 315cm pastel

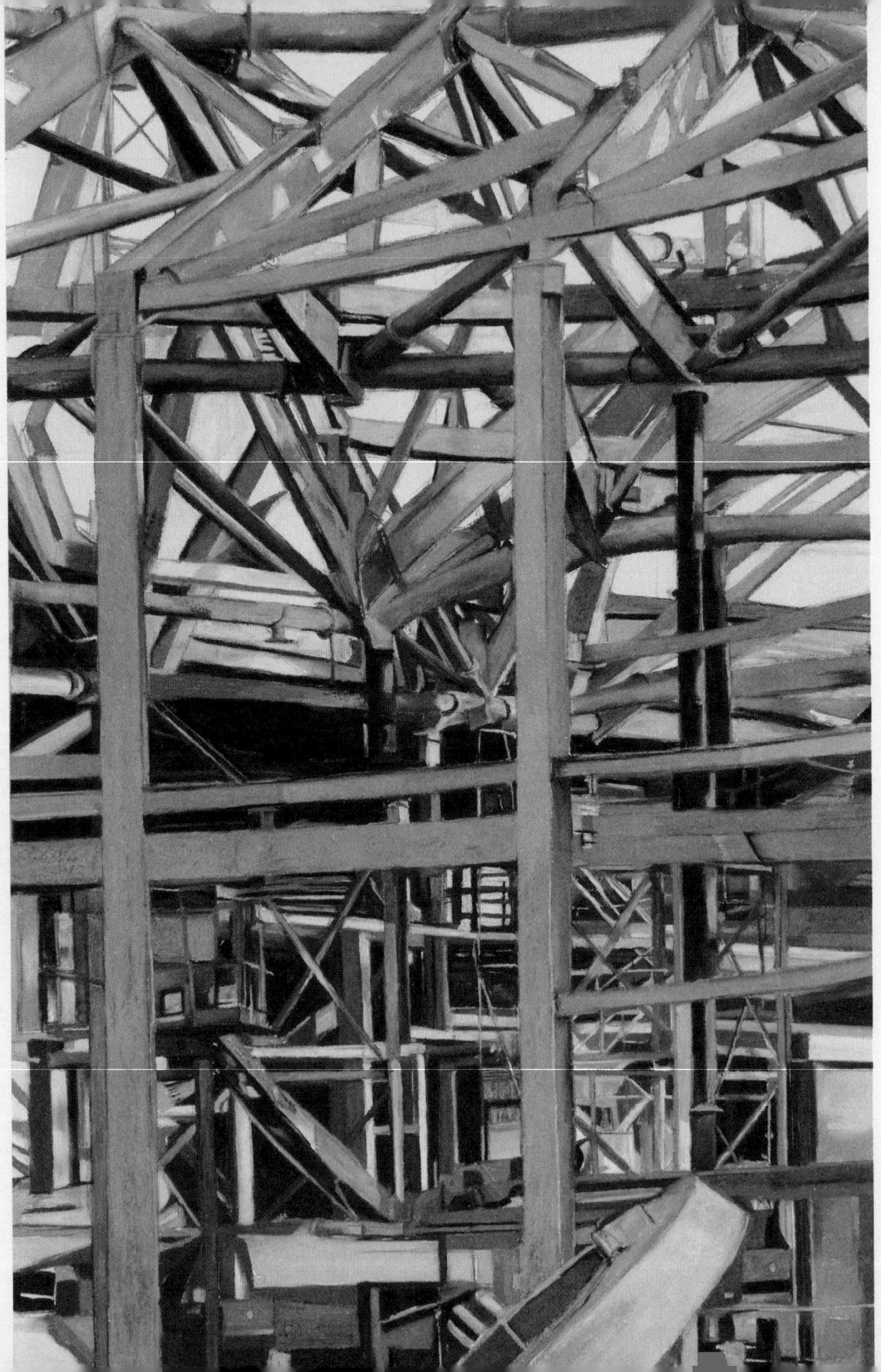

(above)
Steel Contour II (2011)
170 x 105cm pastel

(above)
Steel Contour I (2011)
170 x 105cm pastel

1.

2.

1.
Riverside Propping I (2011)
30 x 35cm pastel
2.
Meeting Point (2010)
89 x 61 cm pastel

1.

2.

3.

1.
Riverside Scaffolding I (2011)
140 x 122cm pastel
2.
Riverside Scaffolding II (2011)
140 x 122cm pastel
3.
Riverside Scaffolding III (2011)
140 x 122cm pastel

(opposite)
Riverside Triptych III (2011)
170 x 315cm pastel

Connections made through process

Alec Galloway

The glass creation for *Drawing on the Clyde* is a true collaboration, not only of ideas but also of processes.

The work has been produced as an illustration of transparent thinking, and it is through the very transparency of glass that we can hopefully gain insight into the diverse working methods that are unified in one element.

A major factor in the creation of the piece was getting around technical limitations of the material. Unlike metal or wood, glass does not enjoy being bent out of shape. It must be teased and handled with care before it can replicate another form. The process of slumping uses flat glass sheets, which are set over a moulded form and heated to the point where the glass softens and loses its rigidity. When this process is controlled, the glass can be formed according to the shape of the moulded form beneath it.

Normally, glass artists spend hours making plaster moulds to inform the shape of the glass, but we used rolled metal sheets produced by Fergusons Shipyard, Port Glasgow, as mould and former, as if we were making the curve of a new ship's hull. In doing so, we united two processes and crossed the boundaries between shipbuilding and glass making.

The metal plates were rolled before being coated with a clay/plaster wash, and then placed in the kiln in preparation for the glass sheets. Each metal form received a glass strip, which was slowly brought to a melting point, before slumping into the metal form and taking on the shape of the curved metalwork. Once formed, our glass sections were ready for the next part of the collaborative process, drawing.

It seemed appropriate to refer back to the architectural plans for the Riverside building itself, as there are distinct nautical parallels between some of the elevations of the building and the blueprints displayed in the archives relating to the plans of many Clyde built ships.

The final process in the work was making these lines and marks of information part of the glass construction. The glass was etched through the process of sandblasting, a technique that uses an aluminium oxide abrasive to mark the surface of the glass. These carefully controlled marks/letters/lines were etched into the glass surface, creating a strong narrative of information, instantly altering the translucence of the glass skin. When projected light is cast through the glass, the etched elements create dark shadows where the sandblasted glass refuses to let the light through. In contrast, light is able to pass through the clear un-etched areas, forming light pools on the floor beneath the work. These light pools and shadows echo the lofts where sections of ships were drawn out by loftsmen, so called because the loft was where they drew curves and calculations, marking out the forms to be cut from metal to create the shape of a ship. Lofts we visited still contained all the information relating to the radii of curved metal forms, and the long strips of wood pegged out to follow the line of the drawing were still there.

Our use of light, casting information shadows, unites this work with the manufacturing skills of the shipyard professionals and builders. The difference is that these shadows and forms falling onto the gallery floor do not speak of a specific vessel but instead of the unique structure that is the Riverside Museum.

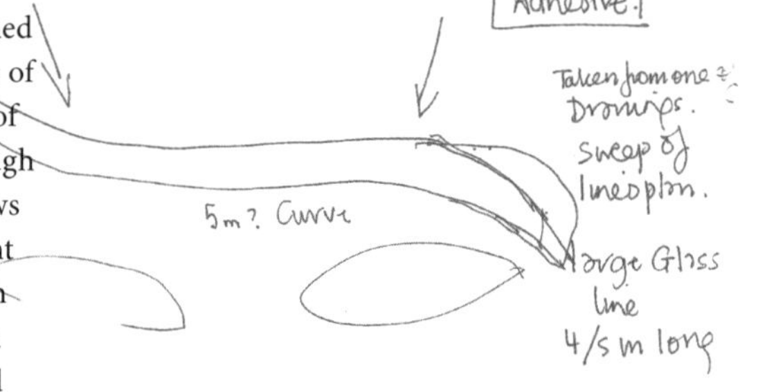

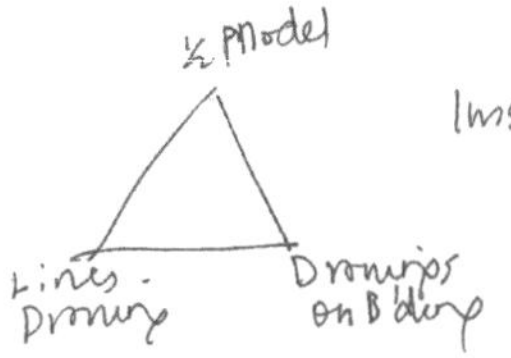

[Handwritten annotations:]
2 sand blasters + Dremel for Drawings.
Glass Curved – Profile in Plaster Glass in section
2/3 Metres
UV Glue Adhesive.
Taken from one of Drawings. Sweep of line of plan. Large Glass line 4/5 m long
5 m ? Curve
Sunderland Glass Centre / Uni. 4m Walk in Kiln.
Glass – Indept. Glass. Alecto follow up. Kiln – Cost
Inscription sandblasting
½ Model
Inscription
Lines Drawing Drawings on Building

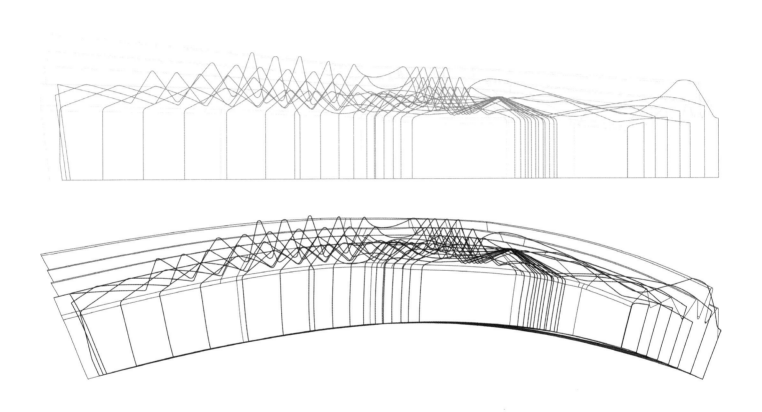

(above)
Line drawing of Riverside #1 & #2
for glass sculpture
Patricia Cain

2.

1.

3.

A Wave of Lines
Ian Johnston

If a ship starts off in the drawing office as a series of inked lines on a two-dimensional plane, these lines took an eventful route through the shipyard before emerging as very real three-dimensional components of a ship.

From a concept in the mind's eye of the naval architect, the precise form of a ship was first recorded in a series of lines that described its beam and length. From the intersection of these two drawing planes, the vessel's three-dimensional shape was determined, though it was still far from expression in tangible form. Drawing these lines was the work of draughtsman who used specialised drawing instruments and flexible steel rules to set up and draw each line. Once the line had been set up, which could take some time, the draughtsman charged his ruling pen with Indian ink and drew it down the ruler to leave a single crisp line. Other lines were added to make what looked like a wave of curves defining the ship from bow to stern. In this manner, a series of drawings or a lines plan was made, containing all the information necessary to enable steel to be formed and a ship built.

The process of converting these lines into steel began by taking them to the mould loft. Here, the draughtsman's scale drawings were increased in size to full-scale by the loftsman who re-drew them on the mould loft floor, which was, in effect, a very large drawing board. Once the lines had been laid off on the floor, forming a colourful and complex network of information, a wooden template was made which accurately recorded the detail of, for example, the curved line that would eventually become a ship's frame.

This curve, now recorded in wood, left the relative tranquillity of the drawing office and mould loft to enter the noise and clamour of the steel working sheds to be confronted by the frame bender. The curve was again transformed, this time from wooden template to a chalk line on a series of massive steel beds lying on the floor of the shed. A series of steel pins was inserted into holes in the beds to follow the chalk line exactly. As this line was being set up, a length of steel section was heated in a furnace to white heat and, when ready, brought out and placed onto the beds. The glowing steel was quickly pushed into the pins to take up the shape of the chalk line and 'dogged' with pins on the other side to ensure that it remained true, as the steel cooled and contracted.

The line had become a steel frame, ready to be punched with holes to accept rivets and taken to the building slip for erection. The line that had started in the drawing office was now a very real and exact part of the ship.

1.
Draughtsmen at work in a large drawing office using a variety of implements, including ruling pens, T-squares and set squares. Half-hulls are fixed to the walls at left.
2.
Setting up a curve. To draw this line on this plan, a thin metal strip which will guide a pen has been aligned to the correct curvature and held in position by heavy weights.
3.
The Mould Loft where the ships' lines were laid out full size on the floor. This loft was almost 100 metres long. A wooden template can be seen on the floor, matched exactly to the line of a ship's frame.

Being Spatial / Spatial Being
Lorens Holm

1.

I have an image of Trish Cain reaching over and lifting a photo out of the photomontage pinned up next to her and pasting it into the drawing she is working on, a drawing the size of a small room, and then layering over it with new marks, new media: drawing and painting and other photos, and building a complex layered atmosphere. Space as texture, supersaturated. It tastes of chalk. The montage was built of photographs of Zaha Hadid's Glasgow Transport Museum under construction; the construction of the drawing recapitulates the construction site. Marks on paper coalesce to form a structure; structure coalesces to form marks on paper. This is more than an affinity between the drawing and the building. Drawing and building form a continuum. We can define a new form of site praxis that brings drawing and building and being into a single traversable field or textural surface. Something new is generated that lies between drawing and building, reducible to neither.

If you watch Cain work, you see that she creates an expanding field. The first mark could have entered the field anywhere (the enduring mystery of origins), subsequent marks expand outwards in all directions. Each line is a response to the one that preceded it. Colour enters in many different places at once. Colours are recalibrated. There is a dialogue of positive and negative. We are in the realm of abstraction. The drawing captures the building at a moment in its construction. It asks us to see, not the illusion that the building will remain in that moment, but – like Piranesi's Carceri – that continuous flux is its defining moment. A particular zigzag truss is lifted to its fixing points. The building section is an extrusion that varies continuously along its length. The space it makes is always under construction.

The work of Cain is about how to be in space: being spatial, spatial being. We create space as we go. Each of us occupies space by making more of it. It raises the question of how we engage with our world. We lean into it with scalpel and pencil raised, rather than sit back and look at it. Construction is the essential part of being in the world, because our world is always under construction. Being in the world (what Heidegger called dwelling, but let's strip dwelling of the Heideggerian whiff of origins) is a matter of engaging in a continual process that constructs it and ourselves and is not just a matter of looking at something that is already fully constituted, from a position – mine, yours – that is already fully constituted. We are all already drawers and builders.

The difference between drawing and building is elided in Cain's work. Either the drawing and the building are equally space, or they are equally representations. A lot is at stake. Our simple and precious category distinction between the object and the picture of the object begins to crumble, and in this dizzying and incredibly creative moment where Cain is poised, everything is possible.

2.

1.
Riverside Triptych III (2011)
Detail of the under-drawing
2.
Riverside Triptych III (2011)
Detail of first layer
3.
Riverside Triptych III (2011)
Detail of Panel 2

3.

Abstracted Material
Rosalind Lawless

Throughout the collaboration my intention was to respond intuitively to the building. Sitting where the River Kelvin and the Clyde meet, on a curve of the Clydeside, the building responds seamlessly.

Colossal in scale, the building sits almost inside out, where solid flat areas of wall meet the curvature of the roof. I was interested immediately in the flat solid wall areas along with windows and doorways. At the beginning of the project we worked from photographs of the construction. These were transferred to photo-positives for screenprinting onto different materials found at the site. Through this process it became apparent that this method was too controlled. From this, we allowed ourselves the freedom to use our natural approach, but with one constant: the subject that we were responding to. Whilst making the work I was aware of the process of constructing and how integral this was to the resulting image, although no longer visible. Hopefully the final images convey this construction.

The focus of my work is intimately connected to the history of the making. The journey of making is part of the work. This became very apparent when working on this collaboration. I was conscious that I was using hand drawn and cut out stencils as a way of building up layers, then stripping them away after printing to reveal a transparent layer of ink that would eventually become the finished piece. Screen-printing is a process I have been working and experimenting with for almost ten years. I work intuitively, responding to what went before; nonetheless, there is a certain measure of learned reaction that lends itself to the way I work.

Working on this collaboration has given me a sense of freedom that I don't always allow myself, and working alongside Trish has eased the pressure in the decision making that comes at the end of a body of work. To have this extra voice has been invaluable. The collaboration has allowed us both to discuss and restate our subject and interests to each other. To have the opportunity to make in response to another artist has been most advantageous. I believe that working together in such a close way, where at points we have looked at the same photograph and then reinterpreted it, has been very exciting, as it confirms not only to each other but also to ourselves where our interests lie and perhaps how we as artists conceive our subjects.

The defining aspect of the work has been the relationship between printmaking and architecture. Working alongside another artist has highlighted areas of printmaking that I have not yet explored, areas that I have looked at again with a different eye. By using transparent layers of colour in my screenprinting I wanted to allow the workings underneath to be visible. This shows the process and journey that went before, demonstrating the link between artwork and building.

(opposite) **Confluence II** (2011)
55 x 45.5cm screenprint and tissue paper on paper

- All material says something diff about how the thing is –
  Interirity/Fragility – differentiation
  Thats why collage : solid + not solid.

- Material describes the thing it is….
  It is the material.

for printmaking
- Material describes the work
  For B'ldng – Zinc Makes what it is .

(this page) Photographs of materials on site

Words for how Materials Meet Up.

Junction
Convergence
Collision

Overlap
Join up – bring together
Joint/juncture
Meet/Meeting/Meeting Point
Junction
Convergence
Collision
Contact
Tough
*confluence (of rivers)
Cohesion
Consolidation
Tightness
Closeness
Union
Coalition
Association
Connection/connecting
Touching
Assemblage
Unification
Bringing together
Stitching
Fastening
Attaching
Annexing
Affixing
Fixing

grafting
merge
inserting
incorporate
anchor
embody
tether
lump-together
stick-on
dovetail
frame
fit
drive in
set
enfold
wedge
interlock
grip
bolt
engage
bond
screw
solder
combine
nail
fuse
merge
rivet
cement
unify
clamp
lace
arrange
clinch
knit
secure
sew
knot
pin
hitch
stitch
bend
buckle
lash
do-up
cast-on
plug in
graft
earth
couple
interconnect
weld
link
suture
bridge
seam
span
splice
hook
hinge
fasten
intersection
harness
Crossroads
twine
Unite
twist
Conjoin
truss
Couple
strung
Yoke
rope
Pair
shackle
Match
swathe
Associate wrap
Moor
roll-into-one
ally

1.
Varla Cladding (2011)
122 x 80cm
screenprint and pastel on paper
Rosalind Lawless

2.
Merge (2011)
76.5 x 50.5cm
screenprint and pastel on paper
Patricia Cain

3.
Bond (2011)
76.5 x 57cm
screenprint and pastel on paper
Patricia Cain

4.
Column (2011)
122 x 80cm
screenprint and pastel on paper
Rosalind Lawless

5.
Plateau (2011)
39 x 39cm
screenprint and acrylic on paper
Rosalind Lawless

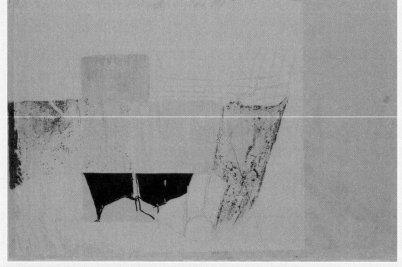

2.

1.

3.

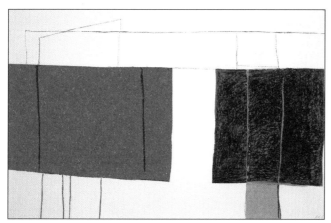

4.

5.

Nothing is fixed, nothing is final...
Phil Lavery

As I write this, nothing is fixed, nothing is final, there is only the process. A process that started with an email, a meeting and an idea.

I liked the idea.

Ideas can take form in many ways. Some can just spring into being, but more often it is necessary to explore the bounds of the possible, and when working with technology, the possible may only be limited by time and money.

There was precious little of either.

And so, the one idea gave birth to others, the amazing, the astounding, the completely impossible, along with the boring, the safe and the done before. Research, tests and trials either ruled things out or transformed them into something new, and still there was potential to go further. Then came the point to apply the restrictions of the physical space, the limited resources and the rapidly passing time.

There were hard decisions.

The more novel technologies were put to one side. We needed the security that at least something had the potential to work. And so we went from six displays to two and, even yet, this could become one. But then, this was never really about the technology ... It is about that idea, the decisions we have made along the way and the risks we are still taking.

There is still a chance that nothing will work.

The end result could be an empty space on the gallery floor or a room with nothing in it. Would that be so bad? The original idea would remain. Pure and uncorrupted by our attempts to bring it to life, it would retain all of its potential.

When doing our projects with schools I always say, it is the process that counts, and I truly believe this. So whatever transpires, thank you, Trish.

The process happened.

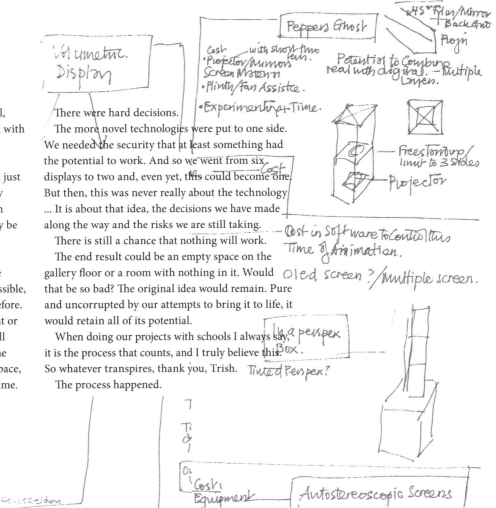

(opposite) **Nothing Finished** (2011)
A frame from a lighting test, created with
Maya 3D by Phil Lavery & Patricia Cain

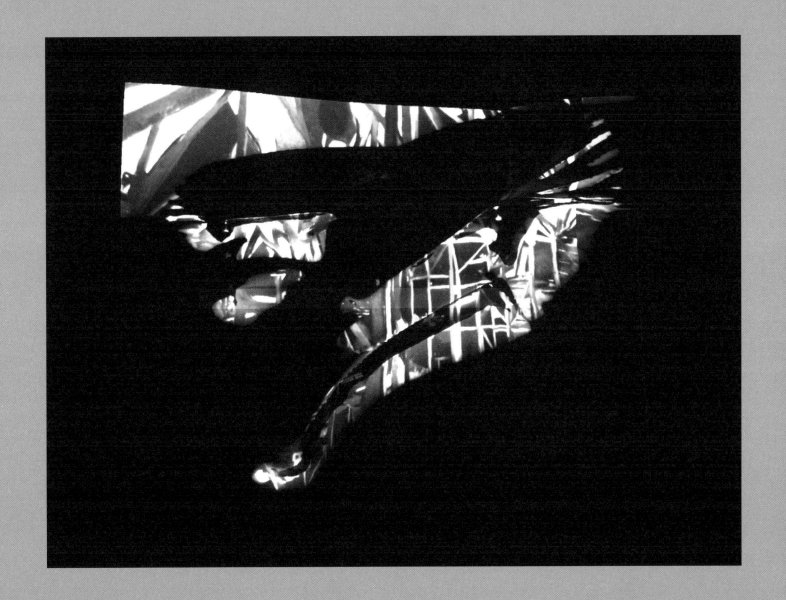

Benefits of drawing by hand in a digital age
Professor Alan Dunlop

'The mother art is architecture' *Frank Lloyd Wright*

I contend that hand drawing is fundamental to the mother art. It is a critical act in the process of thinking and of conveying ideas from the brain to the page. Yet very few architects now draw by hand; they rely on the computer. In architecture schools, the instant SketchUp tool has replaced the drawing board. For many students the computer generated image has become their only means of communicating. Through technology a building can take shape quickly and can look very real. It can be varied, printed, coloured and cut and pasted before you know what you are doing. In my experience, students today know less about the practical realities of how to build than they did twenty years ago. This is a direct consequence of the focus on and the fake authenticity provided by the computer.

Why has this happened? Drawing by hand is tough; you need to practice and to have discipline. It is hard to begin a new drawing, and usually the first marks on the paper are hesitant and show both tension and uncertainty. It takes confidence to put your ideas directly onto paper, the process of hand drawing needs to be taught, and students need to be supported in their efforts. It takes time.

When I draw, I find that the act itself is a means to consolidate my thinking on practical issues for the building: where will the light be, what should be solid or void and, most importantly, can this idea exist in the built sense? Students should apply themselves to this discipline as a basic skill, and schools and teachers who avoid drawing are doing their students a disservice.

Hand drawing should have intrinsic value. It should be an effort of artistic production – the delivery of a drawing worth having. No computer generated image gets close to the spirit of a great drawing. The output of great architectural draughtsmen, Paul Rudolph, Frank Lloyd Wright and Mackintosh, have specific distinction and style that attests to the quality of their thinking as well as their artistic capacity. Their drawings have become iconoclastic because of the duality of their approach and are clear testimony that no effort in preparatory analysis is wasted. Through hand drawing you can learn everything about architects, the degree of rigour and research that they bring to their projects, their attitudes and their sensitivity. It is no overstatement to suggest that line drawing represents the stain of the true architect's soul on paper.

(opposite)
Glasgow Harbour No.2 Cream (2007)
84 x 59cm pen

1.

(left) **MacKay's Boatbuilders II** (2010)
61 x 61cm pastel and pencil

Reflections on the River
Neil Baxter

The River Clyde has long been a focus and symbol of Glasgow's progress. The Riverside Museum's very name celebrates its location alongside what, for centuries, was Glasgow's main transport artery and communication route. The museum and the exhibition which spawned this publication mark the continuous process of change along the Clyde and in the vibrant city through which it flows.

In Glasgow's earliest days, when the nascent city was a place of pilgrimage, the River Clyde was an easily forded outer edge to the lower town. Small boats on the river, fishery rather than trading vessels, were little more than one- or two-man skiffs or coracles. There was a toll bridge in medieval times, but, given the ease of wading across or even driving cattle through the stream, many visitors chose to avoid this levy. Bishop Rae's mid-fourteenth-century bridge replaced a wooden bridge at the south western extremity of the town, roughly in line with the present day Stockwell Street. The Magnum Pons trans Cludan was a twelve-foot wide, eight-arched structure. Much altered and amended, it stood until the mid-nineteenth century, when it was replaced by the present day Victoria Bridge.

By the mid-eighteenth century, Glasgow had quite a different river from the early wide and shallow stream. The engineers John Golborne, James Watt and others scoured and deepened the Clyde to create a navigable channel, enabling goods to be brought right into the heart of the city. The river's banks were lined with a rich variety of structures, some late medieval, others, like the Customs House, fine, if modest, Georgian.

The explosion in Glasgow's industry and the concomitant, extraordinarily rapid growth in the city's population of the Victorian era radically transformed every aspect of the rather douce and attractive little town. Industrial might brought factories, warehouses and homes on an industrial scale. Mass production created the components of radical new works of engineering. The giant structures of the railways thrust right into the heart of the city, everything in their path being demolished to make way for the gods of steam.

The Clyde was a wider, deeper river, crowded with steam vessels. A ticket could be purchased for leisure trips 'doon the watter' or much further afield, indeed as far as Paris, for business. The great industrial sheds of Broomielaw and Tradeston thronged with the clamour of stevedores. Further west, the many shipyards employed thousands of workers. From Govan to Gourock, the Clyde, at peak production, produced a remarkable twenty percent of world shipping.

The visual delight of a home on the banks of the river is a contemporary craving. However, the first part of Glasgow's first new town at Carlton Place is a magnificent row of elegant stone dwellings, connected to the thriving commercial heart of the city by one of two single span pedestrian suspension bridges, the other connecting the Gorbals to the Green. All along its length in the mid-nineteenth century, a cacophony of trams, horse-drawn buses and carts transported the citizens of the million plus conurbation about their business.

Since the mid-twentieth century, the scene is once again radically changed. New apartment blocks clad in glass and aluminium, office buildings on a similarly grand scale and elegant pedestrian walkways now line the river. Recent bridges have restricted the size of vessels on the Clyde. No longer dredged, the river has silted up, and navigation is restricted to boats of very modest draught. Yet the Clyde is still there, right at the heart of the city, a symbol of Glasgow's progress and the continuous process of its evolution. The River Clyde, always beautiful, has always been the focus of delight, innovation, reinvention and simply pleasure for Glasgow's folk.

1.

2.

3.

1.
Holy City (2010)
122 x 91.5cm oil
2.
John Brown Tenement II
(2010) *81 x 61cm oil*
3.
Singer Street / Hill Street II
(2010) *61 x 81cm oil*

Making Spaces
Steve Rigley

In the early stages of designing this catalogue Trish passed on to me a CD containing a batch of technical drawings. Once opened in Photoshop they revealed what looked to be various sections sliced through the hull of a ship, each one meticulously detailed in line and ink. And suddenly I was back in Thatcher's first term, and my first job.

I had left school at 16 to join the drawing office of a large civil engineering firm as trainee teaboy. It was like being catapulted into a kitchen sink drama. The gloomy office was found at the end of a narrow, winding staircase and was occupied by two rows of drawing boards, each lit by an anglepoise lamp and separated by a naughty calendar. And here a dozen or so middle-aged draughtsmen maintained a focused, quasi-monastic silence, broken only by fervent bouts of whistling when a job was going well. For a school leaver it was thrilling to realise that the physical world of bridges, dams and viaducts was somehow conjured up from within this very space, this secret society of clutch-pencils, cardigans and tobacco.

Once I had proved that I could make the tea and fetch the fags, I was introduced to my drawing board. It was roughly the size of my bed. After a couple of days of wrestling with it, I had figured out the various levers and pedals, and, perched on my swivel chair, was ready to offer my contribution. Yet over the next few weeks and months I quickly realised that this amounted to very little. Given the opportunity to draw, my hands became like clumsy boxing gloves within which paper buckled and creased, ink spilt and pencil lines smudged. Then there was the challenge of trying to converse in a new, highly complex visual language that seemed to insist upon concealing the architect's intent.

Unfortunately for some, Mrs Thatcher was to stay in her job for a good deal longer than I, who was out within the year and didn't look back. That is until now, where patched-in behind my firewall it is easy to smirk in hindsight, to sentimentalise and ridicule the office with one phone and the dusty cellar with a thousand rolls of embalmed directives. Compared to my toolbar in Photoshop, the various scale rulers, French curves and pens that I have kept from that time seem crude and uncanny, like implements from some covert masonic ritual.

A little later on, Trish had another CD for me. This one contained photographs of oil paintings. In contrast to her other work, these captured buildings in varying stages of demolition: torn gables, ripped bedrooms and kitchens precariously hanging over piles of rubble and twisted wires. Violent and elegiac, these paintings seem to offer a sober reminder that we can only occupy a temporal space. Design technology is only one detail in the picture, the freeze-frame between the residual and the emerging, the half-broken and the half-built.

(opposite)
Dumbarton Road, Dalmuir (2010)
61 x 74cm oil (detail)

1.

2.

1.
Napier Street looking West
(2009)
81 x 61 cm oil
2.
Deconstruction Study V
(2010)
81 x 61 cm oil
3.
Crown Avenue (2010)
81 x 61 cm oil

3.

(above)
Clyde Redevelopment 12B (2006)
140 x 70 cm mixed media

Acknowledgements

This exhibition has only been made possible with the support of a large number of people who have helped realise my ideas.

Firstly, thank you to Glasgow Museums for the opportunity to exhibit at Kelvingrove Art Gallery, particularly to Anne Perry who has given constant support throughout the project, Charles Bell, Hugh Stevenson, and Sean McGlashan amongst many others.

Thanks to Paul Weston and Bam Construction for allowing me to go on-site during construction. None of this would have happened without the considerable time, help and patience provided by Paul Jaffray and Will McElhany.

To my collaborators, Ann Nisbet, Alec Galloway, Phil Lavery and Rosalind Lawless: thank you for taking the risk and answering that first phone call or email. Ann in particular has constantly lent so much time and support to the project.

The funding of this project has always been problematic and without the considerable support of the various sponsors, so many aspects of the exhibition would not have been possible. Thank you to Fergusons Shipyard, Varla, Arts and Business Scotland, Sam Cartman, Wessex Glass, TruVue, The Bet Low Trust, Clydebank Rebuilt, Elmwood, GalGael Trust, Paterson Timber, The Norma Frame Foundation, Independent Glass, the Ballast Trust, A D Associates, McKay Flooring Ltd, Caledonian Plywood Company Limited, John Watson Printers, Screen Chem, AMK and Unison Pastels.

Many thanks to Ian McNichol of Glasgow Print Studio, whose kind help in the etching project has just been lovely, and to Solveig Seuss and Isla Pedrana for translating their interest in the project through their film-making abilities.

I have been guided and learnt a lot from the considerable experience and special help that was given to me in relation to the drawings projects by both Duncan Winning of the Ballast Trust and Ian Johnston, and by Jimmy Cosgrove at so many other crucial junctures. Thank you also to Joshua Brown for his fabulous technical expertise and help in managing the architectural installation and to Allister Burt for his support with this also.

This lovely publication would not have been possible without the editing skills and discursive feedback of Rowena Murray, the vision and skill of Steve Rigley and the photographic expertise of Lorna MacParland. Thank you also to Zaha Hadid, Lorens Holm, Alan Dunlop and Neil Baxter for their interest and written contributions to the publication.

There has been so much to organise on the ground, and I could not have done this without the considerable assistance of Yiru Wang, Rachelle Carswell, Andrew North, Li Sha, Bi Bo, and Ella Shimmin – you have just been so kind and helpful.

Finally and most importantly to my husband Sam, who has not only put up with me talking about the Riverside for a good few years, but has latterly allowed our house to become nothing more than a studio with a kitchen and bathroom attached, has framed all my work, notwithstanding his own art practice, and has listened and discussed when required – I owe you (again!).

ARTIST

Patricia Cain
Trish Cain is an artist, writer and researcher with a particular interest in the relationship between drawing and thinking. She is the 2010 winner of both the Aspect Prize and the Threadneedle Prize.
www.patriciacain.com

COLLABORATORS

Alec Galloway
Alec is a practising Architectural glass artist, lecturer at Edinburgh College of Art and operates from Cara Glass, an independent studio producing works for both public and private sectors. His works can be seen throughout the UK, as well as USA, Canada, Australia and the Middle East.
alec.galloway@tesco.net

Phil Lavery
Founder and CEO of the Digital Learning Foundation educational charity, Apple Distinguished Educator and Visualisation Consultant, with a previous life as an Architect and Designer.
www.digitallearningfoundation.org

Rosalind Lawless
Rosalind Lawless has exhibited extensively worldwide. Permanent collections include Aberdeen Art Gallery and Pallant House Museum and Art Gallery. Awards include the Tim Mara Award, Royal Scottish Academy travel award, Glasgow Art Club fellowship and Inverarity Travel award. Lawless gained an MFA from the RCA, London in 2004.
rmlawless@hotmail.com

Anne Nisbet
Ann Nisbet is a transdisciplinary practitioner. Her work employs a process led methodology and situates itself in the realms of architecture. As a practising Architect she has won several awards, including the Grand Prix and Gold Medal at the Rose Design Awards.
www.annnisbet.com

CONTRIBUTORS

Neil Baxter
Neil Baxter is a historian, architectural writer and commentator. As Secretary and Treasurer of RIAS, he is responsible for the Incorporation's management, public, political and business endeavours and special projects.
bionbaxter@rias.org.uk

James Cosgrove
James Cosgrove is an artist, writer and designer who was formerly Depute Director of Glasgow School of Art. He is currently a director at House for an Art Lover in Bellahouston Park. A practising artist, he exhibits widely in national exhibitions and in a number of commercial galleries.
www.jamescosgrove.co.uk

Alan Dunlop
Alan Dunlop is one of the UK's leading architects. He has won over fifty national and international awards. In 2008, he was awarded the Gold Medal in Architecture from the Royal Scottish Academy.
www.alandunloparchitects.com

Dr Lorens Holm
Lorens Holm is Reader in Architecture at the University of Dundee. He runs a Masters year design studio in urbanism and writes about architecture, Lacan, and intellectual culture.
L.Holm@dundee.ac.uk

Ian Johnston
Ian Johnston has written a number of books on maritime themes, including shipbuilding on Clydeside. His yard histories include John Brown at Clydebank and William Beardmore at Dalmuir.
iandjohnston@ntlworld.com

Dr Rowena Murray
Rowena Murray is Reader in Applied Social Sciences at Strathclyde University. Her research focuses on academic writing. She is currently writing with Trish Cain about the thesis writing process.
r.e.g.murray@strath.ac.uk

Anne Perry
Anne Perry, Senior Designer with Glasgow Museums for 10 years: manages a multidisciplinary team, and the delivery of major exhibitions and projects for Glasgow Museums.
Anne.Perry@glasgow.gov.uk

Steve Rigley
Designer, lecturer, and occasional writer, Steve is head of Graphic Design at the Glasgow School of Art. He has taught in China, India and the USA.
www.shadowcabinet.org.uk

Hugh Stevenson
A graduate of Edinburgh University and College of Art, Hugh has been a curator with Glasgow Museums for over 30 years, concentrating recently on Scottish art of the nineteenth and twentieth centuries.
hugh.stevenson@glasgowlife.org.uk

All artwork by Patricia Cain unless otherwise stated

Photography: Lorna McParland
Catalogue Design: Steve Rigley

Printed by: J Thomson Colour, Glasgow

Published by Patricia Cain
Copyright © Patricia Cain
ISBN: 978-0-9568434-0-1

READING LIST

Black, J. (2005) *Form, Feeling and Calculation: Edward Wadsworth – The Complete Paintings and Drawings* Phillip Wilson Publishers, London

Bell, K., Hammer, M., Lawson, J., Lawson, J., Thomson, D. and Patrizio, A. (2000) *Men of the Clyde: Stanley Spencer's Vision at Port Glasgow* The Trustees of the National Galleries of Scotland

Bone, S. (2009) *Muirhead Bone: Artist and Patron* Bayham Publishing, London

Cain, P. (2010) *Drawing: The Enactive Evolution of the Practitioner* Intellect Books, Bristol

Hobbs, R. (2003) *Mark Lombardi: Global Networks* Independent Curators International

Hume, J. and Moss, M. (1975) *Clyde Shipbuilding from Old Photographs* B.T. Batsford Ltd, London and Sydney

Illingworth, J.R. (1987) *Temporary Works and their Role in Construction* Thomas Telford, London

Johnston, I. (2000) *Ships for a Nation* John Brown and Company, Clydebank West Dumbartonshire Libraries and Museums

Marzaroli, O. and McIlvanney, W. (1989) *Shades of Grey: Glasgow 1905-1987* Mainstream Publishing Edinburgh

Moss, M. (1997) *The Clyde: A Portrait of a River* Cannongate Books, Edinburgh

Van Gaasbeek, R. M. (2007) *A Practical Course in Wood Boat and Shipbuilding* Dixon Price Publishing, Kingston Washington

Archive Footage from the Scottish Screen Archive
1 - *Glasgow 1980* [Film ref.0974]
2 - *Seawards the great ships* [Film ref.2230]
3 - *Bombing of the Clyde* [Film ref.0538]
4 - *Scottish Shipbuilding* [Film ref.0395]
5 - *Visit a Shipyard* [Film ref.1270]
6- *Scottish Shipbuilding* [Film ref.0395]
7 - *KH4 VC3631(2)*
8- *Construction of tanker 'Nordic Clansman'* [Film ref. 2448]